Ocean Friends

BOTTLENOSE
DOLPHINS

Caitie McAneney

PowerKiDS
press.

New York

Published in 2016 by The Rosen Publishing Group, Inc.
29 East 21st Street, New York, NY 10010

First Edition

Editor: Caitie McAneney
Book Design: Katelyn Heinle

Photo Credits: Cover, p. 1 Yory Frenklakh/Shutterstock.com; cover (series logo coral vector design) Koryaba/Shutterstock.com; back cover mycteria/Shutterstock.com; pp. 3–24 (interior coral vector design) etraveler/Shutterstock.com; p. 5 aabeele/Shutterstock.com; pp. 6, 24 (snout) Pannochka/Shutterstock.com; p. 9 Sokolov Alexey/Shutterstock.com; p. 10 Willyam Bradberry/Shutterstock.com; p. 13 vkilikov/Shutterstock.com; p. 14 Elena Larina/Shutterstock.com; p. 17 Targn Pleiades/Shutterstock.com; p. 18 Neirfy/Shutterstock.com; p. 21 Andrew Bain/Lonely Planet Images/Getty Images; p. 22 A_Lesik/Shutterstock.com; p. 24 (squid) Rich Carey/Shutterstock.com.

Library of Congress Cataloging-in-Publication Data

McAneney, Caitie, author.
  Bottlenose dolphins / Caitie McAneney.
     pages cm. — (Ocean friends)
  Includes index.
  ISBN 978-1-5081-4165-5 (pbk.)
  ISBN 978-1-5081-4166-2 (6 pack)
  ISBN 978-1-5081-4183-9 (library binding)
  1. Bottlenose dolphin—Juvenile literature. 2. Dolphins—Juvenile literature. I. Title.
  QL737.C432M235 2016
  599.53'3—dc23
                              2015023502

Manufactured in the United States of America

CPSIA Compliance Information: Batch #BW16PK: For Further Information contact Rosen Publishing, New York, New York at 1-800-237-9932

CONTENTS

Bottlenose dolphins are playful ocean animals.

snout

Bottlenose dolphins have a long **snout**.

Dolphins breathe through a hole on their head.

Bottlenose dolphins live
in groups called pods.

A baby dolphin is called a calf.

Bottlenose dolphins talk to each other. They make many sounds.

Bottlenose dolphins eat fish and **squid**.

Dolphins can jump high in the air!

Dolphins like to follow boats full of people. They ride the waves.

People can train dolphins
to do tricks!

WORDS TO KNOW

snout

squid

INDEX

WEBSITES

Due to the changing nature of Internet links, PowerKids Press has developed an online list of websites related to the subject of this book. This site is updated regularly. Please use this link to access the list: www.powerkidslinks.com/ocea/dol